Contradictions from an Uncertain Silence

emmett wheatfall

Fernwood
PRESS

Contradictions from an Uncertain Silence

©2025 by Emmett Wheatfall

Edited by John Sibley Williams, R. V. Branham,
and M. F. McAuliffe

Fernwood Press
Newberg, Oregon
www.fernwoodpress.com

Printed in the United States of America

Cover and page design: Mareesa Fawver Moss
Cover art: Tom Coe
Author photo: Tony Sibley

ISBN 978-1-59498-152-4

To all the poets who dare speak their mind poetically,
valuing the liberty
codified by free speech and are willing
to suffer the consequences associated with what is said and written.

Contents

Foreword 9

When the Time Comes for You to Speak 13

What of Me Knows Not..14

For as Long as We've Known 15

Contradictions from an Uncertain Silence 16

Inside America..17

In America [the other way] 18

My Mother's Right of First Refusal.......................................19

I Am Not Jewish—Yet..20

The Face of Your Nation 21

On the Walkways 22

Dissonance in America 23

If the 45th President Is Reelected 24

A Nod to Contempt..25

All That's Ever in the Middle 26

Wherever Americans Are 27

In America, Unsafe Is Everywhere...28

In My Country 'Tis of Thee..30

Under the Colors of Flag..31

Free Speech Has Never Been Free 32

A Child of Two Worlds 33

PRIDE..34

Langston Hughes Told Us How...35

America's End..36

Title Index 37

First Line Index...39

Contents

Every word has consequences.
Every silence, too.

—Sartre, Jean-Paul

Foreword

I first met Emmett Wheatfall in February 2020, at a Milwaukie Poetry Series reading at the Ledding Library, just outside Portland, Oregon. I wanted to put some material on the display table. Emmett treated me kindly, showing me where his books were and how *Gobshite Quarterly* could also be accommodated. I am M. F. McAuliffe. I'm co-founder and -editor of *Gobshite Quarterly*, a multilingual magazine based in Portland. My husband, R.V. Branham, is the founding editor.

In March 2020, I returned to the Ledding Library for another poetry series reading, this time of poetry in Arabic and English. *Gobshite* has, through the years, published some Arabic work; I went to hear new work and possibly new writers. Emmett was there. This time, I encountered his generosity: he presented me with a copy of his new book, *As Clean as a Bone*. I had no cash. "No, no," he said. "It's a gift."

During the first lockdown and its reinstitution and during later COVID surges, Emmett read in Zoom sessions. In 2021, I heard him read Robert Hayden's "Those Winter Sundays," which I had only seen once on a small poetry list-serve. It's rich and precise and austere. Emmett's voice amplified its richness.

R.V. and I had decided that, during COVID, we would publish single annual volumes of *Gobshite Quarterly*—the pandemic having destroyed schedules everywhere, including our translators'. We were proud to have Emmett as one of the contributors to our 2022 issue and delighted to have him as one of the writers at the launch of the issue in May. The whole reading featured great and seasoned voices, but Emmett closed it out magisterially with poems by Monika Herceg and Tomislav Marijan Bilosnić, as well as his own.

—M. F. McAuliffe

To say that "Emmett Wheatfall lives in Portland, Oregon where he writes, records, publishes, and performs poetry" fails to catch the humility of his presentation or the illumination this book of poems brings to the subject of being a Black man in America now—anger and sorrow and grief and rage,

> America / am I your left foot / your shoeless left foot
> / when shoed / I'm without lace /
> —from "In America"

Conditions of being conscious that are unimaginable unless the color of your skin says you must suffer them. On inheriting the racial, social peril of Emmett Till:

> I named my son Jonathan. The weight of bearing the name Emmett
> is too long. Emmett Wheatfall Sr. and Emmett Wheatfall Jr. are
> enough in the Wheatfall family. I took it upon myself to cut loose
> that lingering noose
> —from "My Mother's Right of First Refusal"

The sense of a brewing, growing possibility of pogrom, the return of those Jim Crow laws that were the models for the Nuremberg laws, the massacres that preceded Kristallnacht:

> I've never been to Tulsa, Oklahoma
> The broken glass has been swept away
> And the fires have been extinguished
> Lingering is an uncertain silence
>
> I sleep with one eye open
> —from "I Am Not Jewish—Yet"

10

The sense of being betrayed by false promises: "The Face of Your Nation"; the sense of being unsafe everywhere—"Wherever Americans Are," "In America Unsafe Is Everywhere." And again, the sense of growing threat:

> today
> *insurrection resurrected,*
> *reminiscent of an infant lifting its head*
> *upon waking*

—from "A Nod to Contempt"

These poems illuminate us all. Long may they shine.

—R.V. Branham

When the Time Comes
for You to Speak

When a moment is not yours, you must know it.
When the time comes for you to speak, you must.
When the occasion establishes itself, you must
respect it metaphysically. When in the universe
there comes alignment of providence, settle into it.
When the moment is not about you but someone
who has died violently, remember to reverence
the moment. At that moment, a reverend is not
needed—just a poet.

What of Me Knows Not

What of me can define America? Of customs
and traditions, her manifest history is preserved
in literature, film, and photography. Who am I
to speak of these things and to make light of those
matters of consequence, resting upon laurels
of American penchant for its contrived narrative?
Have mercy on me, America. Have mercy. And to think
myself to be American. As such, what of me knows not.

For as Long as We've Known

*Judge a man by his questions
rather than his answers.*

—Voltaire

A wise man came from a faraway place
to tell the people what they needed to know.
To the wise man, the people replied,
*We have been here for as long as we've known,
and if you do not know how long that has been,
anything you must tell us is not worthy of
our knowing. For you know of nothing
we need to know.*

Contradictions from an Uncertain Silence

This 4th day of July begins its end
I await its sunset to settle in
At twilight gunshots begin to ring out
They are not in salute to liberty
Just humankind's disregard for rule of law
Not respecting spilled blood of patriots
Who did so founding their America
Wherein I'm a descendant of slaves
And unequally yoked with white men
When this 4th day of July ends

Inside America

Is there an inside to America? Is that question far-flung? I've tried all my life to find acceptance, America. To you who have kept your foot wedged against the door,

> I know who you are
> and who you have been
> and who you continue to be.

The passkey I've been given is faulty. My place has been in the kitchen rather than America's living room. Langston Hughes wrote a poem expressing such sentiment.

I don't want to be like Obama. I want to be me and inside America.

In America [the other way]

America / am I your left foot / your shoeless left foot /
    when shoed / I'm without lace /
walking the cobblestone streets of America /

feeling awkward / without balance / do you not see me limping /
    stop looking [the other way] /
lying to yourself / us / we / all-the-while knowing /

I am your left foot / I am / your left foot / shoeless left foot /
    of all sizes / sockless in our society /
I am America / in society / an American / and shoeless

My Mother's Right of First Refusal

My name is Emmett. My full name is not Emmett Till. It was not until I reached the age of moral consciousness, indignation, reason, and rage that Emmett Till's killing was instilled in me.

My mother never stuttered telling me. She exercised her *Right of First Refusal*, refusing to inform me first about Emmett Kelly, the clown, Emmett, Idaho, sheriffs in Westerns named Emmett, and a host of first-name Emmetts.

Her admonition was serious sentiment. She articulated her sentiment in a manner conveying her expectation I be obedient. She knew it was sage admonition that I, having been told about my namesake, am not to forsake the knowledge of my namesake, and to never whistle at a white woman.

To *be small*.

My mother was blunt and upfront. We Wheatfalls, living in the South, my mother being from the South, knew what she was talking about. I listened. I paid attention. I never forgot. I've never whistled at white women.

I named my son Jonathan. The weight of bearing the name Emmett is too long. Emmett Wheatfall Sr. and Emmett Wheatfall Jr. are enough in the Wheatfall family. I took it upon myself to cut loose that lingering noose.

I Am Not Jewish—Yet

I am not Jewish—yet

Since when have I ever been
    They, them, those people
Who shout, *Jews will not replace us!*
They have not come for me—yet

My people have known pogrom too
We have known broken glass and fire
    Most often accompanied by
No less than death and destruction

I've never been to Tulsa, Oklahoma
    The broken glass has been swept away
    And the fires have been extinguished
Lingering is an uncertain silence

I sleep with one eye open

        I am not Jewish—yet

The Face of Your Nation

We opened our doors and windows to you
We Kurds waved when you came to our aid
We poured you tea and served you bread
We bequeathed our trust and loyalty to you
> Our
> Sons fought—gallantly and sacrificially
> Husbands spied, translated; were your chameleons
> Children slept peacefully with you in other rooms
> Our eyes viewed you as brothers and sisters in arms
> How
Should we answer your treachery
Can we set aside your betrayal
Might we ever cheer the face of your nation
Will we ever see you as a kindred spirit
> If we
> Survive the coming ethnic cleansing
> Cannot find refuge in the arms of another
> Unbury our children from unmarked graves
> Ever look back at you Americans
> We will
Never entertain the innocence of your children
Hold suspect your creeds and exceptionalism
Take your apologies like fallen leaves
Turn our backs to your call and extended hand
> Never forget
> We will rise from this our fresh grave
> We will remember we did not wave when you left
> We will recall your poet, Langston Hughes
> I am the darker brother—I will
> Eat well and grow strong

On the Walkways

As the Americas go, so goes the US.
All the while, South and Central America
are watching as the US turns from
    liberty, justice, egalitarianism
    to totalitarianism, tyranny, fascism,
    sedition, and insurrection.
Who among us would even imagine
such things? Is the US destined to be
no more? Is before drying like raindrops
on the walkways that comprise our
once great nation? Is patience treading
water, wading knee-deep in the pools
of contradiction? Keep watching.

Dissonance in America

You think what you want.
It may not be enough.
Outpaced is goodness. Evil's stride is a step and a half faster.
Uttered curses are difficult to recall.
Imagine a flicked match.
Let ensuing flames loom large in your mind.
America's democracy ablaze.
Autocracy outpaces liberty.
Is let freedom ring now a doorbell rather than the Liberty Bell?
Bellum, bellum, bellum!
When was the last time the eagle was seen flying?
You think what you want.
It may never be enough.

If the 45th President Is Reelected

we will not have knocked the meteor out of the night sky
will we have punched a hole in that *Founding* piece of paper

A Nod to Contempt

today
insurrection resurrected,
reminiscent of an infant lifting its head
upon waking from sleep.

insurrection is a nod to contempt.

not every patriot is a freedom fighter.

January 6, 2021, I see them

as dissidents noted for their vitriol
and their attempted coup. And,
for the false narrative proffered as fact
asserting a "stolen election."

now you know.

      now you know,

now, you know.

All That's Ever in the Middle

My arrival to this land was by land
Among a caravan of immigrants who knew not the sea
Who seized not upon the smell of salty sea
We women, children, and men

I'm taught pilgrims came by way of sea
Crowding hull of seafaring vessels carved from trees
They wanted to spill dirt from their hands
While kneeling on bended knee

Is there something to be said for before and after
Wisdom knows who's coming or going
Are the first truly last and the last truly first
All that's ever in the middle should be shared

Go back to your country!

That land is too far and away
And the sea too choppy to breach
America is our home now
America—our home

Wherever Americans Are

In the United States, Americans worship
at the altar of the gun. Willie Nelson was wrong.
There are more than seven Spanish angels.
The communion cup is shared by many.

From sea to shining sea, gunpowder is the
salt of the earth. Single shots are not heard around
the world but in neighborhoods of the poor
and now the affluent. Affluence of violence is
something everywhere, and everywhere is
wherever Americans are in America.

In parks, parked cars in front of homes,
neighborhood schools, elementary, middle schools,
and high schools. And to think Kent State's
active shooter was once a big deal but a footnote
in history now.

And to think the US Capitol Rotunda is not safe.
For the first time in my 65 years of life, I saw with my own
eyes the presidential motorcade. He was accompanied
by an army of gun-toting law enforcement officers.
And to think I have been placed on *HOLD* when I've
dialed 911.

Me? I can only imagine how unsafe I am as I reside
in my RING security protected home.

In America, Unsafe Is Everywhere

I went to a big parade
—Not anticipating the need to flee
Other people died there

At a public park
—I found myself dodging bullets
One almost grazed me

Standing on my porch
—I witnessed a drive-by shooting
The police never responded

Ex state prisoners say
—*Prison is a violent place*
I've never been incarcerated

My fenced-in property
—Rarely stops trespassers
Graffiti appears like public art

US Capitol buildings palatial
—Surprisingly subject to insurrection
Men with long guns have rampaged

Schools, public and private
—Every active shooter's field day
Children tremble under desks

US Secret Service details protect
—Unaware the president may attempt
To choke one of them when incensed

I am a Black person
—Some Black people I fear too
It is a feeling I can't stomach

And them white supremacists
—Who march wearing pure white masks
Proclaiming Jews will not replace us

I shake my head, America

Given the contradictions from
Our shared uncertain silence

I vigorously shake my head

In My Country 'Tis of Thee

In *My Country*,
'Tis of Thee
I'm still not free.
Far be it from me
is my *Sweet land of liberty*.
I've lost the will to sing
Of thee I sing.
Yes, *Land where my fathers died*,
and I'm still not free.
I'm a descendant of slaves,
so I know nothing of
the *pilgrims' pride*.
Black bodies
if stacked
rise *From ev'ry mountainside*.
I for damn sure am not free.
Let freedom ring
from the cracked Liberty Bell
in Philadelphia.
I live in the broken state
being the United States
where here
I'm still not free.

Under the Colors of Flag

Bones are buried / At the foot of Old Glory /
She / Her / Hers / He / Him / His /
They / Them / Are everywhere in America /
Waving / Red / White / Blue / Flappable /
The way big sea billows roll /

Close your eyes, America / Dried bones decay under
the colors of flag / The colors of Old Glory / Listen to the slaves
singing / *Swing low* / *Sweet chariot* / *Coming forth*
to carry me home /

At the foot of Old Glory are dirt mounds / All over
the South are graveyards / Nat Turner is buried in one /
The likes of Emmett Till / The "Tulsa Race Massacre"
is another / All the while, we Negroes still want to be free /

We've been told to slow our roll / Old Glory has got to
widen freedom's road / Too many have died before they lived /
Our eyes want to look up to the glory thereof /

Free Speech Has Never Been Free

In scarlet wrinkles, there is ridicule.
    With scorn comes lashes to persona,
For every person wears a mask.
    Lapel-pinned poppies appear silent,
Whenever spoken will come rebuke.
    Why would anyone want to appear
disheveled at their wedding? Any morsel
    of cake on a tux inexcusable. If on
a wedding dress—for certain tears.
        Free speech has never been free.
Of what worth is death without liberty?
    Who insults a king with impunity?
Miranda Rights are not a rebuke
    and are never keyed in white font.
Sometimes, it feels good to curse.
    And facial wrinkles are forever.
Let the drawbridge down so that
    fresh air may find its way through.
They who are angry should STFU!

A Child of Two Worlds

You will always be a child of two worlds.

—Sarek, (father of Spock)
Star Trek the motion picture

You know you are of mixed race
Black coffee mixed with white cream
Caramel-coated and latte-looking
        A child of two worlds
In the garden of humanity, you are beautiful
Every blossom knows itself
You are not an island unto yourself
Moreso, you are a bridge
Between your mother and me
Between dark and light
Twilight
The shade long before sunset
The sunshine between dawn and dusk
You light up my brown life
You darken your mom's white life
In the garden of humanity, you are beautiful
I love you little blossom
You, the twilight in my life
You are a contradiction from
An uncertain silence

PRIDE

In America
Patrons enjoy PRIDE today
All wide-eyed with wonder
Full of PRIDE that freedom feels free
Asked was a small donation
Seven dollars the sign read—that's all
Imagine that
For a little slice of equity and inclusion
With that multicolored rainbow overhead
And a fresh rain

Langston Hughes Told Us How

I am the darker brother.
They send me to eat in the kitchen
When company comes,
But I laugh,
And eat well,
And grow strong.

   —"I, Too" by Langston Hughes

We are not asking you for access to the table and seats
Despite promise we have every right to be seated
Observing how there are insufficient numbers of seats

We cannot go back to the kitchens from where we came
We will not return to those fields we toiled to churn again
Let the seas be damned before we are sailed as slaves again

White America, you've tried your best to placate us
Nestled us between white breasts that refuse to nurse us
To Black America, given no rest from the toils within us

We choose now to ask nothing more or less of you
We find you lacking in persuasion and asserted proof
The US Constitution, be it water deprived of liquid proof

What Black America has strived for is to be one with you
Once upon a time, we straightened our hair to look like you
Educated ourselves so we would be wholly accepted by you

After decades, Black America finds her pursuit vain
It's a three-card monte in the form of a shell game
We've been fools believing we could win at your game

It's time for us to take big steps away from your table
No worries, Black America doesn't want to turn the table
We will chop, carve, and sand beautiful new tables

White America, Langston Hughes told us how

America's End

Who will pen America's end?
Will it be the right hand? Will it be
the left hand? Will a number 2 pencil
erase cancel culture? Who will edit
the manuscript and approve the
galley copy? Who will publish that book?

Will there be a market for it?
Probably not. Who bothers to read today
anyway? God forbid! The book gathers
dust on some bookshelf. Think about it.
This poem is not written using cursive
writing. Who will pen America's end?
Who will pen—America's end?

Title Index

A

A Child of Two Worlds 33

All That's Ever in the Middle 26

America's End 36

A Nod to Contempt 25

C

Contradictions from an Uncertain Silence 16

D

Dissonance in America 23

F

For as Long as We've Known 15

Free Speech Has Never Been Free 32

I

I Am Not Jewish—Yet 20

If the 45th President Is Reelected 24

In America [the other way] 18

In America, Unsafe Is Everywhere 28

In My Country 'Tis of Thee 30

Inside America 17

L

Langston Hughes Told Us How 35

M

My Mother's Right of First Refusal 19

O

On the Walkways 22

P

PRIDE 34

T

The Face of Your Nation 21

U

Under the Colors of Flag 31

W

What of Me Knows Not 14
When the Time Comes for You to Speak 13
Wherever Americans Are 27

First Line Index

A

America / am I your left foot /
    your shoeless left foot / 18

As the Americas go, so goes the US 22

A wise man came from a faraway place 15

B

Bones are buried / At the foot of Old Glory / 31

I

I am not Jewish—yet 20

In America 34

In *My Country* 30

In scarlet wrinkles, there is ridicule 32

In the United States, Americans worship 27

Is there an inside to America? Is that
    question far-flung? I've tried 17

I went to a big parade 28

M

My arrival to this land was by land 26

My name is Emmett. My full name is
    not Emmett Till. It was 19

T

This 4th day of July begins its end 16

today 25

W

We are not asking you for access
    to the table and seats 35

We opened our doors and windows to you 21

we will not have knocked the
    meteor out of the night sky 24

What of me can define America? Of customs 14

When a moment is not yours, you must know it 13

Who will pen America's end? 36

Y

You know you are of mixed race 33

You think what you want 23